MW01093123

A Healing Legend:

Wisdom
from the
Four Directions

by
Garry A. Flint
and
Jo C. Willems

NeoSolTerric Enterprises
Vernon, British Columbia

Library and Archives Canada Cataloguing in Publication

Flint, Garry A., 1934-
A healing legend : wisdom from the four directions / by Garry A.
Flint and Jo C. Willems.

ISBN-10: 0-9685195-3-9
ISBN-13: 978-0-9685195-3-0

1. Self-actualization (Psychology) I. Willems, Jo C., 1953- II. Title.

RM723.A27F55 2006   615.8'92   C2006-902134-1

First printing: September 2006

Disclaimer
The reader assumes entire responsibility for what he or she may do with the information presented here. The material in this book is experimental and is based on clinical results. There has been no peer-reviewed research proving the efficacy of this treatment method.

The authors offer this information with the clear understanding that the information presented here is not a substitute for professional mental-health or medical advice. If the reader wants mental-health advice or any other professional advice, he or she should seek the services of a competent professional.

Printed in USA
Lightning Source Inc.
La Vergne, TN

Acknowledgments

Garry A. Flint

Thank you to First Nations Elder Patrick Adrian for giving me a valuable gift that changed my spiritual and professional life. I thank Roger Callahan, the developer and principle teacher of Thought Field Therapy (Callahan, 2006), who taught me the treatment method he discovered.

I also want to thank all the patients who were my teachers while I developed the Process Healing Method (Flint, 2006). I especially want to acknowledge the patient who first showed me that it was possible to do Callahan's external treatment method internally without conscious involvement.

Garry A. Flint and Jo C. Willems

We are grateful to Jason, Ryan, and Joy Haxton, Denise Farmer, Donna Cameron, Joan Davidson, and Margaret Peterson who read and critiqued the book as we developed it. We also want to thank Christopher Butler of WordsRU.com who offered significant editing suggestions for the manuscript and Claudia Volkman of Elance.com for the final proofreading.

Contents

Introduction

This little book was designed to teach your inner-self a treatment process that can heal many of your emotional issues. The authors present the treatment process metaphorically through a delightful tale about a boy who has problems with his thoughts and a schoolyard buddy. How did we come to write this book?

Teaching the inner-self how to treat personal issues is the basis of the Process Healing Method (Flint, 2006). Flint discovered this treatment process in 1993 when using a treatment method called Thought Field Therapy (Callahan, 2006, Craig, 2006). In Callahan's method, a person taps on acupressure points while thinking about an emotional issue. From Learning Theory, it is easy to explain this tapping as a learning process. The tapping speeds up change by replacing negative emotions associated with an old painful memory or issue with neutral to positive emotions experienced in the present. Process Healing takes this tapping one step further by teaching a person's inner-self to do the actual treatment.

During the twelve years of using and developing the Process Healing Method, Flint occasionally noted an interesting outcome. Some of the individuals who received treatment reported that they noticed positive changes beginning to happen to those around them—the spontaneous transfer of the treatment process. Obviously, communication without spoken language was possible. People could, in some way, share the treatment process with others.

Recently, a First Nations Elder told Flint that before the 1900s Elders used to communicate in a manner that didn't involve spoken language. After meetings, they would disband and do what they agreed on in their unspoken communication. This idea caught our attention. We started thinking about alternative ways to teach the healing process. Storytelling was a natural vehicle for this.

We wrote *A Healing Legend: Wisdom from the Four Directions* to teach the reader's inner-self this treatment process to move him or her in a positive direction. It is not meant to be a substitute for professional help. In addition, it is a way to explore the truth that useful healing wisdom can innocently pass between family and friends. The reader can wonder if he or she can share the treatment process with others in the same way.

People's reactions after reading the story suggest that this little book made a significant impact on their lives. While this may not be true for everyone, we believe that many readers will experience positive life changes after reading A Healing Legend: Wisdom from the Four Directions.

Garry A. Flint
Jo C. Willems

A Healing Legend:

Wisdom
from the
Four Directions

A Story Before the Story

THINGS change, that's the way it is in the mountains—that's the way it is everywhere. Sometimes things in nature change very slowly and cannot be easily seen, like the trees growing in the forest. Sometimes things change on a regular basis, like the day-to-day living of a squirrel and baby birds growing up. Sometimes things change very quickly, then settle to a new way of being and don't change for a long time. That is where our story begins...

A long time ago, a great glacier covered the peaks and valleys of a mountain range. For thousands of years, the movement of the glacier ice wore away the loose soil and softer rock along the highest crest. Eventually this created the towering rocky walls of a circular valley near the top of one of the peaks. When the glacier melted at the end of the last ice age, the ragged stone walls of the cirque were revealed, making the peak look a lot like the indented crown of an old-fashioned ranger's hat.

Winter and spring, the water on the walls froze and melted repeatedly, breaking off many chunks of rocks. Most of the chunks of rock that fell away got caught up in the soft soils of the alpine meadows or rolled farther down the mountain where they became stuck behind trees or other rocks. And there they remained, seemingly unchanged forever. However, some of the largest chunks rolled all the way down to the bottom of the valley and ended up in the riverbed.

Over time, the flow of the river water changed the stones. Some were worn as smooth as the inside of a bathtub. Some of them rolled around in the current until they were broken into pebbles, then into even smaller pebbles and finally ground to sand, all the while moving further down the stream. In this way, a goodly amount of the mountaintop, mostly in the form of fine sand and silt, had traveled all the way to the ocean. And the ocean was hundreds of miles away.

Then, on no particular day, one large boulder cracked off the stone walls far above the valley and rolled down the steep mountainside to settle into a shaky balance on a mess of rubble just above the river. The very weight of the rock's great size held it into place, jammed against many other smaller rocks. It was bigger than a house and leaned at an odd angle, over hanging the valley, where it remained for thousands of years while the rest of the valley, and indeed the world, changed around it.

The broad river valley below the rock was a special place. It was sheltered and faced south, exposing the land to the warming rays of the sun, even in winter. And it was one of the first spots to melt out every spring, making it a good place for all living plants and animals. When this unusual valley was discovered, it became a popular winter home for the first peoples of this land.

The people were special too, having learned to live from what nature offered. Their customs and their ways of doing things were based on knowledge gained through the experience of many generations. Part of that knowledge was the importance of working for the good of all and thus ensuring the survival of the whole nation. For many generations they wintered in this place under the boulder, setting up their lodges year after year. The valley floor offered good grazing for their horses and the forest was rich with game that they hunted for food. Wood was plentiful to build lodges and to keep the fires burning in the short, cold days of winter.

Every spring the people moved on to a new place. It was their way to move about with the seasons. Doing so allowed the winter camp to be cleaned and healed by nature's forces so it would be ready for the next winter. Eventually though, they came no more. Times had changed.

A Kid Named Kidd

Now only one simple square of logs occupied the area under the boulder. The hands of children had created the small structure of piled branches and other debris—a play fort. A lone boy was standing in the center of the fort. He would occasionally crane his neck and stare up at the leaning boulder. He looked worried.

"What if that huge boulder rolled down the hill and crashed into the fort?" he said aloud to himself. Shaking his head, he busied himself tucking bits of grass into the cracks between the logs. He'd learned at school that the pioneers had chinked their log homes in this way. He liked copying the pioneers. His great, great, great grandfather had been a pioneer. Kidd was named after him as his grandfather had been. Kidd's grandfather was a gifted gardener, famous for his roses, and he was also a war hero. Kidd didn't know much about being a gifted gardener, but he thought a lot about being a war hero. That was cool.

Today he was feeling restless and out of sorts. It was one of those 'what if' days. He felt anxious and jittery like he did after watching a scary movie late at night when his parents weren't at home. It was when Kidd felt this way that the 'what ifs' began bugging him—like, what if that great big rock started to roll down the hillside when he was playing in the forest below. He would look at the rock and think, *What if*? But even though he felt this unknown fear, it didn't stop him from playing in the fort he and his friends had built. Today he was alone and the 'what ifs' were even stronger, so strong he could hardly think.

And there were other 'what ifs' that followed him around. What if the monster from the deep came up out of the drain in the middle of the sidewalk when he was walking by the drain? What if he wasn't able to stop the monster and it destroyed his house and all the houses around the neighborhood? What if his mother opened the refrigerator door and the monster was in there waiting? Oh, that one gave him goose bump shivers!

Sometimes Kidd liked the 'what ifs' and the shivery excitement of his imagination and it was fun to think about scary stuff. But today was one of *those* days—the 'what ifs' were giving him the creeps. Sometimes when he felt like this the 'what ifs' bothered him for a long time.

The next day when Kidd went to school, he was still so creeped out by the 'what ifs' that he couldn't pay attention at all. He got into trouble because the teacher asked him a question and he didn't know what she asked him. Then the rest of the kids laughed at him, especially that mean bully Alfred.

At lunch time the kids all called him stupid and then Billy the Kid.

"My name is Kidd," he yelled back at them.

"Billy the Kid, Billy the Kid," Alfred taunted in a very loud voice while strutting around the playground. Everyone was laughing.

Kidd got so mad. He gritted his teeth and tried to count to ten, but Alfred kept circling around him, jeering. Finally, Kidd couldn't take it any more! He pushed Alfred.

Everyone around them suddenly got silent. The ring of schoolchildren dispersed as a teacher approached.

"Kidd!" the teacher exclaimed. "No fighting or bullying on the school grounds!"

"It was a...an accident," Kidd stammered. "I tripped...I..."

"You did not, Kidd. You pushed Alfred."

All the other children were gone, even Alfred. Kidd was alone with the teacher. His cheeks blazed with embarrassment. He looked at the ground and said nothing.

"You're on notice, Kidd," the teacher said firmly. "If this happens again you will be put on report, and you know what that means!" The teacher glowered at Kidd for another moment and then saw Alfred trying to take a little girl off one of the swings. "Alfred..." the teacher called out sharply and walked swiftly in the direction of the swing set.

Kidd felt a prickle of tears behind his eyes. If he was put on report, that would mean the principal and his parents would be involved. Then he would be in big trouble. What if he got put on report, then what? More 'what ifs.' How could he ever explain to grown-ups about the 'what ifs'?

The biggest problem was all this fear that was knotting him up inside. The knots were the reason why he couldn't pay attention in class. He sniffed, then rubbed his nose with his hand. What if he got put on report? He wanted more than anything to ask about that. But how could he talk about it? How could he tell anyone about all the fears that followed him around in his head?

Who Was That?— Who's There?

Kidd thought about the 'what ifs' as he wandered down the dusty trail towards the fort in the forest. After another difficult day in school he was glad to be away from everyone, especially Alfred. He kicked at a rock and watched it hop and roll down the trail ahead of him. He jumped a few giant steps to where it lay on the edge of the path and gave it a might blast with his foot. The rock zinged off the trail and Kidd heard it smack into a tree trunk deep in the forest.

He picked up a second rock and hucked it after the first. He heard it whack against a trunk with an echo that was satisfyingly loud. Then he whipped another rock, with all the force of his throwing arm behind it, and heard the sharp crack as it came in contact with a tree close by before ricocheting off into a thicket of brush.

"Hey!" a voice erupted from a bush at the base of the tree. "Who did that?"

Kidd wrinkled up his face, thinking that it was an adult yelling at him and he would be in trouble again. The voice did sound like an adult, too—a cross adult.

He thought about running away, but just as he turned to go the voice said, "Don't you go running off now. Not after you woke me up so rudely."

"Huh?" Kidd looked at the bush. It was a very small bush. How could an adult be sleeping under such a small bush? "Where are you?" he yelled, feeling a bit scared. What if this adult knew his parents and told them that he'd been rude? Another 'what if.'

"Hey! Where are you?" Kidd yelled out louder. "I can't see you." He moved a bit closer to the bush and then leaned against the tree to peer down into the foliage. "Are you a kid or what?"

There was no answer. He was now really creeped out. He scrambled back over to the safety of the path as fast as he could go. Then he laughed at himself for feeling scared. Stupid bush. There was no one there. Stupid Alfred. Stupid school.

He walked down the trail the way he'd come, kicking rocks and thinking about all the stupid things that bugged him. Especially the 'what ifs.' What if that voice had been the monster of the deep? What if the monster in the refrigerator was waiting to get his mom? What if...?

Kidd ran all the way home and was relieved to see his mother in the kitchen when he got there.

She was already starting to make dinner and was rooting about in the refrigerator. Her head, safely attached to the rest of her, emerged as she carried out a carton of eggs and some vegetables. What a relief!

"How was your day, Kidd?" she asked with a warm smile.

"Okay," he replied as he always did.

"Are you hungry?"

He nodded.

"You can have three cookies."

Kidd reached up to the cookie jar on the counter and selected three cookies. His mother was busy making dinner and didn't watch as he picked out the three biggest ones. He always took the biggest ones first, though they all seemed pretty big.

"Are you going out to play?" his mother asked, smiling.

"Naw, going to my room."

Kidd gave her a quick hug as he passed by.

"Okay," his mother replied as she prepared dinner. "Thanks for the hug."

Suddenly he whipped around and gave her another quick hug just to be sure she was fine before he climbed the stairs to his room.

Kidd felt good when he was in the kitchen beside his mother, but as soon as he sat down on the bed in his own room the 'what ifs' started in again.

"What if the monster really was in the fridge?"

He ran back down the stairs to check that his mom was okay and then opened the refrigerator door just to be sure there were no monsters inside.

"Kidd, what are you doing?" his mother said, her voice betraying a hint of annoyance that was softened with laughter.

"Looking for monsters," Kidd replied.

"What a funny boy you can be," she chuckled. "But I need you to get out from underfoot for a while. Please go look for monsters elsewhere while I'm cooking dinner. I'm sorry I'm so busy now but we can talk later, after dinner, if you want."

"Okay," Kidd replied with a sigh.

Walking out into the backyard, he started playing with his truck and excavator. He pushed the machines around, making roads in the soft earth, but he wasn't paying much attention. He kept thinking about the 'what ifs.' How could he tell his mom about the 'what ifs'? Did she ever have 'what ifs' when she was a kid? Somehow, Kidd had trouble imagining his mom or his dad ever being kids, they were so grown-up now and so occupied with grown-up stuff. The 'what ifs' were Kidd's problem, one he had to deal with himself.

Look Closer, Pal.
Real Close

The next day was Saturday. Kidd had planned to meet some of the other boys from school at the creek where they were going to catch frogs but after they teased him so much the day before, he didn't know that he felt much like being with them. He rode his bike to where they were all hanging out. Standing on the high bank above the river, he watched as the other boys laughed and grabbed at the frogs in the mud along the water's edge.

Alfred spotted him and yelled out, "Hey, are you spying on us or what?"

Kidd sighed and kicked his foot at a clump of dirt along the edge of the bank. It started a small landslide down the hill.

Alfred yelled out, "You trying to kill us or what?" He started to run up the bank towards Kidd.

Kidd turned and raced for his bike a few yards away. It was leaning up against an old cottonwood tree that had once held a tree house. The tree house was now just a pile of old gray boards and broken poles scattered around the base of the big old tree.

Kidd had to negotiate carefully so he wouldn't step on any rusty nails protruding from the debris. That slowed him down enough so that Alfred and the rest of the gang managed to reach the top of the steep riverbank. They could see him running away.

"Look at the chicken," Alfred chanted, clucking and flapping his arms like an angry hen. The others started clucking too.

Kidd grabbed his bike and, after a quick leap through the last of the old tree house junk, peddled away as fast as he could. Who needed them anyway! His mom had told him that he should just get away from Alfred when he was acting that way. Sometimes Kidd wished he could smash him, though. Then his friends would see that he wasn't chicken. What if he did smash Alfred? That was a good 'what if' to think about. Except that he'd probably get into trouble. But it did feel good to think about smashing that bully—it felt really good.

That afternoon, Kidd went again to the fort in the forest to see if the huge rock had fallen down the hillside. It was still perched precariously above the valley floor. Kidd stared at it a while, then decided he would go home and read his old comic books.

He started back down the path. All of a sudden a voice yelled out, "Hey you!"

It was the same adult voice that he had heard the other day. It sounded like a gangster's voice, all gruff and dangerous. It said, "You were here before. You woke me up, then ran out on me."

"Where are you?" Kidd yelled out, looking around. He couldn't see anyone in the forest.

"Jeeze, you dunderhead, can't you figure it out? I'm right here." The voice seemed to come from the base of a tree but Kidd could see nothing there.

"Look closer, pal. Real close. Keep looking— that's it—you're getting warmer, warmer, warmer." The voice laughed, like a good friend who was teasing.

Kidd knelt down at the base of the tree. He stared hard at the ground. He could see some little rocks, a worm that looked dead and a couple piles of dried-up leaves. He pushed the leaves away and, to his surprise, underneath was an arrowhead. It was made of flint, just like he had learned about in school. A real arrowhead!

"Cool," he said, as he reached out for the treasure.

"Hey! Hands off, buddy," the voice seemed to erupt from the dusty piece of flint. "Don't you go messing with your elders. Don't you have any respect for something as old as I am? I'm ancient, you know. I predate Christopher Columbus by a long shot."

Kidd jumped back in fright. Who ever heard of an arrowhead that could talk? This had to be one of those monsters like in the movies. But monsters in the movies were make-believe. Kidd shook his head as if to clear away the cobwebs. He looked down at the arrowhead again.

"Now don't you go running off again like you did last time I spoke to you. At least have the courtesy to cover me back up. It'll be quite a while before the autumn leaves fall again, and I don't like being exposed this way. Could be dangerous, you know. What if something were to happen? What if someone came along, saw me and took me off to a museum? What if something like that happened to me?"

The 'what ifs' caught Kidd's attention. He knelt down to look at the arrowhead closely. Tentatively, he reached out a finger and gently touched the surface of the small piece of stone. "I never heard of a talking rock before," he whispered. "How is it you can talk?"

"Oh, I didn't always know how to talk. A long time ago I was part of that mountain way up above you. That was where I lay for eons, part of a great stone wall. Then one day, an old man who was an arrow maker discovered the stone I came from and carried me down to the valley. The old arrow maker was an elder of the tribe and he knew many things. When I became fashioned into an arrowhead, the elder held me in his hands and then breathed his wisdom into me. Now when someone wakes me up, like you did, I can talk. That is part of the wisdom the old man gave to me. Knowing when someone needs to talk."

Kidd sat back on his heels as he listened to the story. It was almost as though he could see the arrow maker in his mind. His lips formed an "O" as the wisdom from the arrow maker was shared with him.

A cackle of laughter came from the old flint lying at the base of the tree. "What if I was still a rock way up on that mountainside? What if the arrow maker had never found me and breathed his wisdom into me? What if I didn't know when someone needed to talk? Then where would I be?" The arrowhead laughed again.

"Do you know about 'what ifs' too?" Kidd asked. "Do you have weird thoughts about 'what if'?"

"I know all about 'what ifs.' I know about the feelings of being afraid of things that might happen, even though I know that they won't happen. I know all about the 'what if they happen' fears. Is that the way it is for you?"

Kidd nodded.

"Do you want to figure out how to be happier?" the arrowhead asked.

Kidd paused. He had never thought about that before. "What do you mean?" he asked.

"I mean to be happier, so you don't have to be filled with thoughts of 'what if' all the time. Are you interested?"

Kidd felt confused. He felt like running away. He also felt like crying and he didn't know why. It was as if a huge bubble was growing inside, a bubble about to burst. At the same time, it felt good that someone else knew about his secret struggle with the 'what ifs.'

"There is a big difference between what is possible and what is probable," whispered the arrowhead quietly.

Kidd had to lean down to hear him.

"What is possible is about if something could happen. What is probable has to do with how often it happens. Most scary things never happen, or not very often anyway. This is part of the wisdom of knowing the here and now."

Kidd could hear voices from far down the path and became nervous that his friends would see him as they passed by on their way to the fort.

"I gotta go," Kidd said. He carefully picked up a handful of leaves and spread them gently over the arrowhead.

"You will come back again." It was not a question but a statement of fact.

Kidd nodded. Then he doubted that arrowheads could see, so he said, "Yeah, I'll come by again. I come here a lot. I'm kind of glad that I woke you up. You won't tell anyone I was rude, will you?"

"Naw, I'm only gruff that way when I don't know someone. But now I know you. You will come back so that you'll learn some of the wisdom that was breathed into me. You'll come back and share the 'what ifs' with me."

"Cool," Kidd whispered. He could hear the voices in the distance growing louder and louder, so he rushed to brush his tracks away from the base of the tree before sprinting to the trail. When the other boys came up to him, Kidd was casually sauntering along, whistling.

"Hey Kidd, where were you?" one of the boys called out. "Alfred is such a jerk. He didn't come because his mom drove over to the river and grabbed him. He was yelling at her, and she was yelling at him. What a couple of jerks. Are you going to the fort?"

Kidd joined the group heading back the way he had just come. When he passed the tree with the little pile of leaves at the base, he thought he heard a faint sound like someone clearing his throat, a *harummm* sound. It was as if he had a friend looking out for him.

What is Possible and What is Probable—The Story of a Feather

That night Kidd learned that Aunt Melanie and Uncle Stan were planning to come over and visit all day Sunday. Kidd didn't like the thought of Uncle Stan coming over because he always felt a bit uncomfortable around his big, gruff uncle. He also knew that he wouldn't be able to go to the forest any time on Sunday. He felt frustrated.

As he got ready for bed on Saturday night, he was almost too excited. Thoughts of finding the arrowhead kept going round and round in his head. It was too hard to think about going to sleep. He wanted to get back to the forest and make sure the arrowhead was real and not just in his imagination. Somehow he knew that finding the arrowhead was important, and not just for himself. It was hard to think of sleeping.

When he did finally fall asleep, he dreamed about the arrow maker. He could see the old warrior climbing up the steep-sided mountain to the high clear air of the alpine. The old man searched and examined the cliffs all around before selecting the bit of stone he wanted. His gnarled hands carefully chipped away the edges to form the tiny arrowhead. Then the ancient elder of the tribe raised the stone in the palm of his hands and, turning to each of the four directions of the earth, breathed on the arrowhead while whispering words older than mankind itself. The dream made Kidd feel good. It was hard to wait until he could to go back to the forest path.

On Sunday, Aunt Melanie and Uncle Stan arrived first thing in the morning. Kidd's mother bustled about in an excited manner.

"Today is a special day for the whole family," she said as she led Uncle Stan and Aunt Melanie into the living room where Kidd was sitting on the couch.

"Yes, it is," Aunt Melanie replied. "Today the whole family and lots of other folks are going to honor Great Aunt Linda." She turned to look at Kidd. "Do you know who Great Aunt Linda is?"

Kidd nodded. "We visit her all the time. She's very old," he replied.

Aunt Melanie laughed. "Indeed she is. She's turning ninety years old today. Aunt Linda was a school teacher, did you know that?"

Kidd nodded.

"She was a wonderful role model for many of her students, myself included," Aunt Melanie went on, as if she hadn't asked Kidd a question.

Kidd's mom left the room for a moment. He could hear her calling up the stairs, and in a moment Kidd's little sister and dad came into the living room.

"Is everyone ready?" Kidd's mom asked.

She came over and checked Kidd's face and neck and hands to make sure they were clean. Then she gave him a quick hug. She bustled over to Kidd's little sister and inspected her, too.

Kidd's dad good-naturedly held out his hands for inspection and everyone laughed. "We're all cleaned up and ready," he said. "Don't worry."

"It's just such an important day," Kidd's mom said with a blush of embarrassment.

"It is indeed. How often do we get to go to a birthday party for someone who is nearly a century old—and such a nice old lady, too," Kidd's dad replied.

"Wow, when you think about it, that is old," Uncle Stan said. "Holy cow! She was born before... well, probably before there were cars."

"Not many around in those days, anyway," Kidd's dad said as they all followed him out to the family van.

Everyone piled in for the drive over to the retirement home where Aunt Linda lived. Many people had been invited, and when they arrived the reception hall was crowded. Kidd was dismayed to discover that he and his sister were the only children present as far as he could tell. He had expected it to be like a school assembly with a lot of other kids because Aunt Linda had been a teacher and her students were coming to the party to honor her. But he couldn't see very many students, just a lot of grown-ups.

He found the party boring. Lots of people who had known Aunt Linda stood up to speak, mostly former students, now grown up. They talked of how she had affected their lives. Along with reading, writing, and arithmetic, she'd taught them values of honesty and kindness that they still held dear today. One man attributed his success as a doctor to Aunt Linda who had taken the time to help him get past a reading difficulty, now called dyslexia. Without Aunt Linda, he didn't know where he would be today.

Aunt Linda sat in a chair right in front of Kidd. Sometimes she nodded her head as though she was dozing, as though she too was as bored as Kidd. Aunt Linda was wearing her best dress hat, which had an enormous feather sticking out of the top of it. Kidd noticed a small frond of the huge old feather was about to fall off. He blew softly, then a bit harder. The feather ruffled and waved. Great Aunt Linda bent forward a bit and coughed. The jerking movement dislodged the tiny bit of feather. It drifted down towards Kidd.

With carefully timed breaths, he kept the feather fragment afloat. He had to be careful not to blow too hard or it would swirl out of reach of his breath. Up it went with a breath, then down it floated. Up again, then down again. Watching the movement was wondrously fascinating.

All of a sudden, the monotony of the speaker's voice changed, and with great clarity Kidd heard him say, "What if that feather drifted slowly down onto Kidd's nose? What if Kidd sneezed?"

Kidd took in a sharp breath and looked up. Everyone was dead silent. He looked around in a panic. Had he really heard the speaker talking about the feather? Suddenly there was a rumble of movement. What if...?

Kidd's heart was pounding under his best dress shirt.

"And so I give you...Great Aunt Linda," the speaker said in a loud voice.

Everyone was getting up to applaud Aunt Linda.

Kidd sighed with relief as he stood up and clapped his hands as hard as he could.

They all remained standing after the applause died down. Someone helped Aunt Linda to walk to the head of the room where she sat down in front of a huge birthday cake. The cake had nine candles, one for each decade. She laughed in her old lady voice as she tried to blow out the nine candles. Even Kidd's little sister could blow out nine candles with no problem, but it took Aunt Linda several tries and much polite laughter.

One by one, the people patiently waited turns to receive a small piece of cake, and then they walked past Aunt Linda to shake her hand or kiss her cheek. When it was Kidd's turn, the elegant old lady ruffled his hair with a gnarled hand.

"My, you are growing up more every time I see you, Kidd," she said.

He hated it when adults ruffled his hair like he was a stupid cat or something, but he smiled and then shook hands with Aunt Linda, real hard, like a man.

"Oh my!" Aunt Linda exclaimed. She winced a little, giving Kidd another smile. "You are a fine, strong lad."

Kidd nodded again and then rejoined his family standing in a group eating their cake.

"Boy, that sure was a tiny piece of cake," Uncle Stan said when they were finally outside of the overcrowded reception hall.

"Lot of people there," Kidd's mom replied.

"Indeed, I was surprised at how many showed up, but then, she is a lovely lady," Aunt Melanie added.

"But they went on and on," Uncle Stan said. "Had a hard time staying awake."

"Stanley!"

Uncle Stanley laughed, and then he said, "Who wants ice cream?"

"I do," chirped Kidd's little sister.

"Me too," echoed Kidd, a bit hesitantly. He really didn't like Uncle Stan, but he did like ice cream.

"But it's before lunch," Kidd's mom protested. Then, at the look of disappointment on Uncle Stan's face, she graciously nodded agreement.

A loud cheer went up as they all piled into the van and drove to the ice cream parlor. On the way the whole family chattered loudly about the party and together they trooped into the store where they stood in line waiting for their treat. Uncle Stan dropped one arm over Kidd's shoulder, but Kidd wiggled out from under it with the pretence of trying to decide what he wanted. Kidd didn't like it when Uncle Stan touched him. Uncle Stan didn't seem to behave like the rest of the adults in his family.

After the ice cream, after lunch and then, after a long afternoon of sitting politely while the adults talked, it was time for dinner, and then finally Uncle Stan and Aunt Melanie went home. Next, it was time for that last half hour of homework. Then it was dark and too late to go out. Kidd breathed a sigh as he waited patiently for the next day after school. It was still a long way off.

Something You Believe Is True Will Be True Unless...

Kidd's mind was on the arrowhead all the next day at school. Fortunately, part of the day was spent talking about North American history before Columbus, so he was very interested. The teacher praised him for his imaginative answers. Not once before lunch did he think of a 'what if.' He only had a few thoughts about 'what ifs' later because Alfred kept calling him Billy at lunchtime. What if that big rock came down when Alfred was in the fort?

After school, Kidd sped off as fast as he could. He knew the guys were planning to catch more frogs, so he felt fairly safe that he wouldn't be followed. He ran up the path through the forest so fast that he ran right past the place where the arrowhead had been. Then he wasn't sure which tree it was. They nearly all looked the same. Finally he saw the small bush and knew he was right. Beneath the tree, the dead worm was still curled up beside the pile of dried leaves. He scooped the leaves to one side. The flint lay as it had for eons.

It looked just like a plain old arrowhead. Cool, but not magic.

"Hey, you there," Kidd whispered.

No answer.

Maybe Kidd had imagined it talking before.

"Hey! You!" he repeated loudly.

Still the arrowhead was silent. Then Kidd remembered that he had awakened it by throwing a rock at the tree. He picked up a rock and knocked it loudly on the trunk of the tree.

"What the...? Who in blazes is waking me up at this time of day? Oh, it's you, is it?" The gruff voice of the flint echoed through the forest. "So you came back."

Kidd crouched down and held his fingers up to his lips to suggest that the flint be a bit quieter and said, "Shush, there might be other kids around here. What if some of the other kids were to come by and hear you?"

"What if they were to see you talking to a bit of rock, is more to the point," the arrowhead said with a chuckle. "What if that?"

Kidd felt a bit uncomfortable at the thought of being teased by the other kids for talking to a rock. What if they did find out about him talking to a rock?

"There is a big difference between what is possible and what is probable," the arrowhead said.

"Possible is what could happen and probable is how often it happens."

Kidd didn't say anything, but just sat hunched down looking at the arrowhead and thinking about the 'what ifs' now starting to form in his head.

"Did you know that inside of you there is the ability to heal what is bothering you?" the arrowhead asked abruptly. The words seemed almost like thoughts inside Kidd's head. As if they had come from inside him, but he knew they had come from outside, from the piece of stone at his feet.

He wanted to say that nothing much was bothering him, just like he did when his parents had those talks with him after dinner. He wouldn't tell his mom or dad what was on his mind because he didn't want them to feel sad or mad. So he kept those things that bothered him the most to himself. With a sigh, he started telling the flint about Alfred and his teasing. Then he added, "How can something inside me stop Alfred from being such a bully?"

"It's tragic, but people who have been hurt often hurt other people," the flint said sadly.

"So, people who have been hurt by others want to hurt other people?" Kidd asked hesitantly.

"Sometimes," the flint agreed.

Kidd thought about what he had just said. He pursed his lips and twitched his nose.

"But I'm feeling hurt," Kidd said. "Does that mean that I hurt people? I don't want to be a bully like Alfred." He felt uncomfortable because he remembered not letting his little sister play with him the other day. That made her cry.

"Have you decided that you want to figure out how to be happier?" the arrowhead asked. "It sounds like you do."

"I've been thinking about it," Kidd said, "but I don't know how."

"You don't know that you know how, but you do. Inside each and every one of us is a part that has been there from the beginning. That part knows how to figure out how to be happier."

"Inside me?" Kidd asked.

"Yep, inside you."

"But how can it help me to feel better about Alfred?"

"That is a belief that's getting in the way."

"Belief?"

"Yes, something that you believe to be true... will be true...until you decide it is false, until you decide differently from your belief. Take the 'what ifs,' they are beliefs that will be true until you understand and sort out what is possible from what is probable. That's how beliefs work. Some beliefs get in the way and stop us from figuring out how to be happier. These beliefs stop that part that has been there from the beginning from doing its job."

"Weird." Kidd scuffed the ground with his shoe as he listened. The arrowhead was talking to him as though he was an adult. He wondered how it was that he was able to understand because he was only a kid. Then inside he realized that 'thinking he was only a kid and couldn't understand' was a belief. The belief was that a kid couldn't understand adult stuff. He knew that wasn't true because he understood everything the arrowhead was saying to him.

"Weird," he whispered again.

 The Arrowhead's Tale of Black Raven

The arrowhead under the tree was silent for a moment. Kidd crouched down, waiting and wondering if the flint would speak again.

"A long time ago, when the first peoples were here, there was a boy, much like Alfred. He lived in the lodge that was just up from where your fort is now."

Kidd looked up through the trees towards the fort. In his mind, he could see the lodges the way they were illustrated in his history book at school.

"The people lived in a cooperative way where every person was important and had value. When something wasn't right with one member of the group, it affected everyone, much the same way we are affected within ourselves when something isn't right."

The arrowhead cleared his voice and said, "You already know all about what it feels like when something isn't right inside."

Kidd nodded slowly, thinking of the anger he felt towards Alfred.

The arrowhead went on, "And you know how this affects your whole way of feeling on the inside and acting on the outside."

Kidd nodded. He did know about these things. He had just never thought about them before in this way.

After clearing his voice again, the arrowhead went back to his story. "The people had a tradition that the grandfathers would raise the grandsons. And it was the same with the grandmothers and the granddaughters. It was this way because it allowed the parents of the children the freedom to do the hunting and the work that was essential for the survival of all. The grandparents taught the children all they needed to know about the ways of the people. In this tradition, the knowledge of the people was passed from generation to generation. The children were raised with kindness and patience."

After a moment of silence the gruff voice went on. "But it didn't always work that way. There was one boy, Black Raven. A disease had killed his grandfather soon after the boy was born. Black Raven's father was a great warrior and was often away from the tribe. Black Raven's mother worked hard gathering food for the winter and preparing the meat and skins brought home by her husband. Neither parent had much time for the upbringing of their son."

"That's kind of like Alfred. He doesn't have a dad and his mom works. Whenever I see her, she is always mad at Alfred. She's mean to him."

"And so..." the arrowhead agreed, "just like Alfred, Black Raven's anger and actions affected the whole tribe. He often attacked the younger children and made everyone feel uneasy. People who act like Black Raven often mess up other people's happiness. There was talk among the women of banishing Black Raven even though he was still so young. The boy's mother felt ashamed but was unable to change her son's ways. He would not listen to her. The boy's father was too great a warrior to be bothered by children's problems and felt angry that not all was right in his lodge."

Kidd thought about how hard it must be to not have a dad. He loved his own dad and always wanted to spend time with him. Alfred must be hurting a lot not having a dad.

The voice of the arrowhead broke in on Kidd's thoughts. "The old arrow maker who created me saw what was happening and was troubled by it. He climbed up to the base of the big rock, which still hangs above the valley, and made a small fire. He placed medicine grass on the coals and breathed in the medicine smoke of the sweet grass. With one breath he breathed in the direction of the heart. The next breath was drawn from the direction of knowing. He then breathed to the direction of the body's power. The last of the four directions was of healing. He breathed the longest in this direction as he prayed for guidance."

Kidd looked up at the big rock and then turned in the four directions of the compass as he listened to the arrowhead. He felt the same magic, as though he was standing beside the old arrow maker.

"The arrow maker then lay down under the shadow of the great stone and fell asleep. In his sleep, he came to a place were the eldest of the elders could be found, and he asked the ancient one what to do about Black Raven. The eldest of the elders drew the smoke from the four directions and then, after a long time, replied, 'Black Raven has much pain. It is as if his hurt and pain are like the gopher holes in a field of beautiful wildflowers. You must send him out to fill in gopher holes.' Then he stood up and said, 'You must all fill in gopher holes. You all have gopher holes to fill in.'"

"What did he mean by gopher holes?" Kidd whispered, but the flint went on without answering. He too was caught up into the memories of another time.

"The arrow maker fell into an even deeper sleep as he lay down beside the fire in the lodge of the eldest of the elders. He dreamed of a large field where the children of the tribe were playing. Gopher holes dotted the field and the children tripped and fell as they ran around in their games. Then he saw the gopher holes were being created by Black Raven's hurt and anger. All that hurt and anger was messing up everyone's happiness."

"Then what happened?" Kidd whispered, half to himself.

"In the dream the people learned how to fill in their gopher holes. As they filled in the gopher holes, their anger towards Black Raven was less. Because of that, Black Raven also learned how to fill in gopher holes. As the angry boy learned to heal the anger pitting his life and causing hurt for others, he learned he was able to be happier. He learned that the tribe valued him as highly as it valued anyone else. In time he became a warrior, then a great warrior, respected by all the people."

A long silence stretched out into the afternoon. Kidd wondered if the arrowhead had fallen asleep again, but then it started to talk. "The arrow maker's sleep became very deep and dreamless. When he woke up he could not remember having gone to the eldest of the elders, but he had the sense that he now knew what to do about Black Raven."

The arrowhead fell silent again. Kidd was eager to hear more of the story. He waited but the old flint didn't speak. Kidd thought about tapping on the tree trunk with a rock to wake the arrowhead but decided not to. He carefully gathered up some dried leaves and twigs and gently covered the tiny bit of stone. Kidd felt quiet inside, but puzzled, as though something had happened, but he didn't know what.

Some gopher holes are bigger than others. Some are huge. The really big ones have to be filled in a little bit at a time, working here and there around the edges. Eventually they become like little gopher holes that can be filled right in. It is usually done that way.

Metaphor for subconscious/
unconscious (other than
conscious) healing

It Was Kidd Who Was Different

The next day at school Alfred was behaving the way he always did. It was Kidd who was different. He wasn't afraid of Alfred any more. He could see how hurt people sometimes do hurt other people, and Alfred was hurting a great deal. When Kidd looked at Alfred, he could see that he was really very lonely and acted in those stupid ways because he was unhappy. Kidd thought of Black Raven. He and Alfred were a lot alike. When Kidd was talking to Alfred at lunchtime, the name Black Raven slipped out. Alfred immediately accused Kidd of calling him names.

"Hey," Kidd defended himself against Alfred's angry words, "I didn't call you names. I called you a name, but it's a good name. It's the name of a great warrior chief."

"Huh?" was Alfred's response. He stopped yelling and looked at Kidd. "Who was that?"

"Someone I heard about. When he was a kid his grandfather died and his father was too busy being a warrior. Black Raven was angry and became mean to everyone, until one day one of the elders taught him some wisdom. After that, Black Raven grew up to become one of the greatest warriors of them all. I was thinking about how much you are like him."

Alfred looked at him intently, a look that Kidd hadn't seen on his face before. Kidd didn't know if he should run or not.

"Is that so?" Alfred said, screwing up his face in wonder. "Where did you hear about him?"

Kidd all at once felt panicky. How could he tell Alfred about where he had heard the story of Black Raven, especially when he didn't even know how he knew part of the story. Just as he was about to make up a lie, he noticed that Alfred wasn't really interested in the details. The bigger boy was hitting his fists on his chest and mimicking a war cry, quietly so as not to catch the attention of the playground monitors who were always on his case.

"I am Black Raven," Alfred said as he strutted around. The other boys watched and were a bit envious that Alfred had such a cool name.

"Let's go play warriors at the fort after school," one of them suggested.

"Yeah," they all agreed. Then they started making up warrior names, but none of them felt as real and as cool as Black Raven.

And His Mother Blinked with Amazement

That night after dinner, Kidd's mom said that she was planning to take the whole family out to Playland for Kidd's birthday the next weekend. He was allowed to invite two of his friends along. Whom did he want to take?

"Just Alfred," the words were blurted out even before Kidd was aware of them.

His mother looked at him with a startled expression on her face. Alfred had been the cause of so much distress for Kidd. It had gotten to the point where she had thought that they should try to move Kidd to a different school.

"Are you sure?" she said. "How come you're hanging out with him now, after he hurt you so much in the past?"

"Mom..." Kidd began, thinking more with his heart than his head. "I know why Alfred is the way he is. It's because he has no friends. The way I see it now, it's like...maybe he needs friends. When he isn't acting like a bully, he is cool. He has great ideas of what to do and stuff."

"Alfred isn't going to lead you into trouble, is he?" his mother questioned seriously.

"I'm not dumb, Mom!" Kidd replied in exasperation.

"No, you're not," she agreed, amazed at the compassion and insight in her son. "You're quite clever and wise for your age."

Kidd looked up at her. He felt warm inside from her compliment.

"So you want to invite Alfred, and who else?"

"I think just Alfred, if that's okay. I kinda want to get to know him, and when we are with the other guys, he often seems to act as if he needs to be a jerk. Is that okay?"

Kidd's mother blinked with amazement and tried to hide a smile of pride. "Just Alfred it is," she said. "I'll call his mother tonight and see if he can come."

10 Really, It's True—That's Just the Way It Is

The next day at school, Alfred was jerkier than ever and tried to include Kidd in his bullying of the other kids. Kidd started to worry that he'd made a mistake. What if Alfred acted this way towards his family?

All at once the 'what ifs' started to bother him. He hadn't thought about the 'what ifs' since the arrowhead had told him about Black Raven. Now he could feel that knot in his stomach again, and he started to worry about Alfred, his family, the stuff at school and that big rock hanging over the fort. "What if Alfred teases my little sister the way he does at school? What if he is rude to my mom? Then what would I do?" Kidd asked himself. For the first time in days, he thought about that old arrowhead in the forest and decided to go and see if it was still where he'd left it under the pile of old leaves. He would do that right after school.

"But what if that big rock were to come down and smash the fort?" he worried. "What if I was in it?"

Part of him didn't want to go back to the forest. Part of him was scared of the rock. But another part of him wanted more than anything to talk to the arrowhead. The arrowhead had a way of understanding what was inside of him. Well, at least he didn't have to worry about the big rock falling down and hurting the arrowhead. There was no way that rock could roll as far as the tree where the arrowhead lay. And the arrowhead was made out of rock, not flesh and bone like Kidd, so even if it did, it would be okay.

"But what if it did? What if that big rock rolled down the hill that far? What then?"

After school when Kidd wanted to slip away to talk to the arrowhead, he saw Alfred the Black Raven waiting for him on the steps of the school. Alfred now acted as though Kidd was his new best friend and always wanted to be with him.

"Hey, what do you want to do today?" Alfred said. "Wanna go catch frogs or something?"

Kidd sighed. "Can't," he said.

"How come?"

Kidd searched in his mind for a reason. He didn't want to tell Alfred about the arrowhead. He scratched his head a minute then stuttered, "Gotta go...to...a...an appointment...yeah, the dentist."

"Oh, how yucky. Oh, poor you." Alfred was all sympathy.

"I gotta go right away."

"I'll walk with you."

Alfred followed Kidd down the street. Kidd started walking faster and faster to leave Alfred behind but every time he looked back Alfred was right there, grinning at him. As it was, Alfred walked down the street behind Kidd all the way to the dentist's office. Kidd had to go inside, sit down, and pretend to wait. Alfred was looking through the glass in the door while the receptionist said, "Can I help you?"

Kidd blushed and held up a magazine he had snatched up from the seat beside him. "Ah... oh, um...no, I just stopped in to look at this for a bit." When he looked at what he was holding up, he turned even redder. It was a woman's magazine on makeup and stuff. And it was upside down!

"I guess I've got to go now," he dropped the magazine as if it were a hot potato and edged over to the door. He could see Alfred walking down the street, back towards the school.

Kidd slipped out of the door and ran through the streets, zigging and zagging in what he hoped was a pattern to avoid being tailed. It was like in a spy book—exciting and fun. He was pretty much sure Alfred was not following him because Alfred had said he was going to punch out someone after school. That was probably where he was now.

Out along the forest path he sped. He could hear the voices of some of the kids at the fort. He ducked into the woods so they wouldn't see him before edging warrior-like up to the tree that was now becoming very familiar. Kidd was beginning to think of this spot under the large tree as his special place.

As he crouched down beside the bush, Kidd noticed the dried up worm was gone. Some creature must have found it and enjoyed it as a snack. Then he saw there was another dried up worm a few inches away from the base of the tree. He could tell it was a different worm because it was longer and red in color. Things change.

It had been quite a while since he had last visited the arrowhead. The pile of leaves had blown to the side, partially exposing the tiny rock. Luckily, it wasn't showing enough so anyone would know that the piece of flint was anything other than a bit of rock. For the most part, unless you really looked hard at it, the arrowhead looked just like a rock. That must be why it had lain so safely under the tree for such a long time.

"Hey!" Kidd whispered as loud as he dared. Then he tapped on the tree with a quiet sharp knock that seemed to vibrate down the trunk and into the ground. He heard a yawning sound and then what might have been a burp! Sounds similar to what his grandfather sometimes made when Kidd woke him from an afternoon nap.

"Hey, are you awake?" Kidd whispered.

"What? What are you saying? What...?" The flint's voice erupted to echo into the depths of the forest.

Kidd wanted to run. He was nervous that the others by the fort would hear. "There are a bunch of kids at the fort. Please be quiet," Kidd said firmly.

"Huh?" The arrowhead replied, still rather too loudly. Then, when more fully alert, the old flint added in a whisper matching Kidd's, "Oh, there are others around again. Why did you wake me then? It must be important given your need to keep things private."

Kidd felt relieved. The arrowhead was good to talk to. But sometimes it was just like any other adult—not too smart at understanding what it was like to still be a kid.

The arrowhead chuckled, as if it knew what Kidd was thinking. "So things have been happening, I take it?"

Kidd nodded and launched into an explanation of how things had changed between him and Alfred.

"Ah," the arrowhead said with satisfaction. "You're gaining some of the wisdom from the four directions and learning some of your own wisdom, too. Very good. Some gopher holes have been filled in, I see. Well, well…"

Kidd screwed up his face and wondered what the old flint was talking about. But then he remembered how the story of Black Raven ended—a weird ending.

"That wasn't the ending," the arrowhead said. "You have discovered that you have some gopher holes to fill in. Did you know that inside you there is a part that was there from the beginning? It has the ability to fill in all those gopher holes. Every time you think of something painful, that part inside of you can find and fill in the gopher holes. Can you feel them being filled in now?"

"Right now?"

"Yeah, right now."

Kidd felt strange, like there was a different feeling in his head. As if his mind was busy doing things without him.

"Did you know all that built-up, out-of-date anger in kids like Alfred changes the here and now? And, all those 'what ifs' you think about change the here and now, too."

"Huh?"

"When you think of the 'what ifs,' do they change the way you act?"

"Sometimes." But Kidd wasn't really sure.

"How about when you can't pay attention at school because of the 'what ifs' in your head—does that change the way you act?"

Kidd nodded and made a face. "I hate being called stupid when I can't pay attention because of the 'what ifs.'"

"Those 'what ifs' are like Black Raven's gopher holes. What if you were to fill in all those gopher holes right now?"

"Right now?" Kidd asked again, a bit puzzled, although what the arrowhead said made sense. It was just so new to think about.

"Yeah, fill them right now—all those bad feelings like anger and the 'what ifs.' We could really call the 'what ifs' fear, couldn't we?"

Kidd nodded slowly.

"Some of those gopher holes are bigger than others. Do you notice that?"

Kidd felt himself nod again. It was almost as though some other part of him was doing the nodding. Weird.

"Those bigger gopher holes take time. You fill in around the edges a bit, then rest and see how it feels. Then, when it is right, you fill in some more and rest again. Eventually the hole gets smaller and more manageable."

"Who's filling those gopher holes?" Kidd asked.

"Inside of you, you have a part that can fill in all your gopher holes."

Kidd nodded again. This time Kidd himself was nodding, and something inside of him was nodding too. He was beginning to understand what the flint was saying. "Is that how Black Raven became a great warrior and leader?" Kidd asked.

"In everyone's life, there are things that cause pain and sadness. When we can fill in the gopher holes, we can use the wisdom that comes later. This is what happened when you stopped feeling so afraid and hurt by Alfred. You could see what it was like for him to be so alone. Your own fear had kept that wisdom hidden from you."

Kidd beamed. He was beginning to see how the story of Black Raven unfolded.

"Alfred," he said slowly, thinking while he was talking, "acted the way he did today because he doesn't know how to have friends."

"Could be," the arrowhead agreed.

"So he needs to learn how to be a friend. Maybe I could tell him that I don't want to hang around him when he is being a bully. I don't want the other kids to think I am a bully too."

"So...that could be," the arrowhead said thoughtfully.

"I never told anyone this, because I was afraid of getting laughed at," Kidd blurted out. "When

I was really little, maybe when I was five, Uncle Stan was tickling me and flipping me up in the air. I didn't like what he was doing and I was really crying, but he thought I was laughing. I wanted him to stop because I had to go to the bathroom, but he wouldn't stop. I remember thinking, *What if I was to go right on him*?"

"Then what happened?" the arrowhead asked with great gentleness and understanding.

Kidd listened for any teasing and laughter behind the words, but there was none.

"I don't remember," Kidd said.

"Bear in mind, the big gopher holes take time. Some of those bigger gopher holes are really yucky, painful memories. Sometimes we get very upset by those yucky memories and we want to forget them. And we can do that too, because when they are really bad memories, after the hole has been all filled in, a bit at a time, you can cover that hole up with leaves and stuff. Then you won't have to look at it at all if you don't want to. However, you have to remember that all your gopher holes have value. You learn important wisdom from every one of your gopher holes. Wisdom about how to behave towards others and to look after yourself too."

Kidd's brow wrinkled as he thought of what the arrowhead had just said about painful memories. It wasn't all that difficult to understand, though it wasn't the way he usually thought about the painful things in his past. He looked over at the arrowhead again. He didn't say anything but chewed his lip as he thought about how much easier it was to talk about the painful memory of Uncle Stan in this way.

"And there is more," the arrowhead went on. "Even from before you were born there was a part of you that can fill in all the gopher holes. And you can even fill the gopher holes that stopped you from filling the gopher holes before now."

Kidd giggled. The idea seemed funny. To fill in gopher holes that stopped him from filling gopher holes was like something The Three Stooges might say, but at the same time he knew what the arrowhead was talking about.

"Yep, you can fill those gopher holes that stop you from feeling better," the flint said with conviction. "And you know what else?"

"What?" Kidd asked.

"You can do it all automatically."

"Huh? How? How can I do that?"

"It's really simple, that part of you that was there from the very beginning can fill in those gopher holes, even the ones from before you were born."

Kidd could feel things happening inside his head. It was as if he were thinking but couldn't think about what he was thinking. He was confused but it didn't feel bad like the confusion he sometimes felt in math class at school.

"Hey, and you know what?" the flint asked.

"What?"

"That part of you that was there from the beginning can fill in those holes even when you are not paying any attention at all."

"Huh?" Kidd wrinkled up his nose in disbelief.

"Really, it is true. That's just the way it is." The arrowhead said this with deep conviction.

Kidd nodded. "Maybe if I think it is true then it is true."

"Maybe that is true," the arrowhead agreed.

"I'm really tired now," Kidd said. "But I'm not so scared of what Alfred will do on my birthday. If he's a jerk, I will tell him to cool it."

"And if he isn't a jerk, well...there is wisdom to be gained from that."

Silence fell between the two of them, a stillness that was a good feeling. After a long moment, Kidd gathered up bits of leaves and covered the small piece of stone. Then, to prevent the arrowhead from being uncovered by the strong winds that blew down from the cool reaches of the mountain every night, he collected a bundle of larger sticks and created a small, crude hut upon which he piled more leaves. When he was satisfied, he crept back out through the woods until he was out of sight of the fort. Then he scrambled up to the trail and strolled casually along the path to join the rest of the kids playing.

"He must have had no cavities," Alfred roared out as he saw Kidd approaching. His face was beaming. "Did you get a sticker for being so good?"

Kidd felt guilty for the earlier lie that he'd told Alfred. Now the lie was getting bigger. Lying sucked. That must be some of the wisdom the arrowhead was referring to—learning from the pain of making mistakes. Kidd joined the other kids and tried to ignore the banter about the dentist as best he could.

"Dentist appointments suck," one of the boys said, tossing a stick off into the brush.

"Poor Kidd," Alfred whined. "Had to go get his teeth cleaned. Oh! Oh! Poor, poor boy!"

The others laughed. Kidd joined in, and soon the subject of the dentist was forgotten in the fun of trying to construct a log shack in one corner of the fort. The shack kept falling down. At one point, when Alfred was buried in the collapsing sticks and poles, everyone laughed, including Alfred, which surprised Alfred as much as it did the others.

Maybe It Was from Learning about History?

On Saturday, Alfred's mother dropped him off at Kidd's house. Kidd was watching from the living room window and saw their old battered car stop at the end of the driveway.

"He's here," he yelled out to his mom. "Alfred is here."

Kidd continued to watch as Alfred and his mother remained sitting in the front seat. Alfred's mom was on Alfred's case. Kidd could see it on their faces even though he couldn't hear the words being yelled between them as they sat in the car. Alfred then jumped out, slammed the door shut and walked slowly up the driveway towards Kidd's home. Kidd was glued to the window, shocked by the commotion, so different from his own family.

Alfred's mom tossed a lit cigarette out of the car window as she drove off. And she was driving way too fast for a residential area, with children out playing everywhere. Kidd wondered why adults had to behave in such stupid ways, as if they never grew up. He was glad that his parents, for the most part, were not like Alfred's mom. Kidd's mom had said that it was hard to be a single working mother. That was part of the reason why Alfred's mother acted the way she did.

The doorbell rang and Kidd's mom answered it before he could skid off the couch. He groaned inwardly as he heard his mom greeting Alfred warmly, but he couldn't make out Alfred's reply. He prayed that Alfred was not being a jerk. When he entered the hall, he saw that Alfred was all dressed up and clean as if he was going to church. He was holding a present in one hand and he very politely wiped his feet on the mat.

Using his fingers, he pulled his bottom lip up over his top lip and said, "Birthday delivery, ma'am." His lip was flapping as he talked.

Kidd's mom laughed. "Oh Alfred, I had no idea you were such a comic," she said. "Come in. We are going to leave for Playland in just a few minutes."

She turned and saw Kidd standing behind her. "Kidd, show Alfred around while I make sure your sister is ready, will you?"

Kidd awkwardly led the way into the living room and said, "This is the couch and here is the TV. We've got a bathroom upstairs if you need one..." He didn't really know how to show someone around. He had never paid attention to what his parents did when adult company arrived.

Alfred was just as awkward, smiling and nodding as he looked at the furniture and said, "I just went before I left, thank you."

It was all weird. Then Alfred spied Kidd's plastic racetrack set and dropped down on his knees before it.

"Cool," he whispered.

"What is your set like?" Kidd asked.

"Oh, mine's not so big at all," Alfred lied. He didn't have a racetrack set. His mother said it took up too much room. He really wanted one. "I got you a present," he added.

Alfred handed over the small gift and Kidd tore off the wrapping. It was a robot transformer.

"All right!" Kidd exclaimed in pleasure. He pried open the plastic package and twisted the robot transformer through the many movements required to turn the tiny car into a robot and then back into a car again.

"How fast will it go?" he cried in glee as he knelt beside the orange plastic racetrack.

Alfred sat back as Kidd set the car at the top of the track. Both boys watched it shoot down to whip across the floor. It crashed against the couch. They broke into laughter.

"Cool!" Alfred squeaked excitedly. He picked up the car, transformed it and had the robot walk back through the air to the top of the track where he transformed it again before sending it down the looping race course.

The car swooped off the track at a corner and flipped through the air before skidding across the polished wood floor.

"Yikes!" Alfred croaked out, seeing the car come crashing to a stop at the feet of Kidd's mom who had just entered the room. All at once Alfred got very quiet. He looked scared as Kidd's mom picked up the new toy.

She smiled at the boys and said, "This is very nice, Alfred. How kind of you to give it to Kidd. I know that he wanted just such a...thing." The robot arms were sticking out of the race car body making it look like a big bug.

She reached over and patted Alfred gently on the arm, causing him to visibly relax.

"I hate to interrupt your fun, but we're ready to go," she added. "Your dad is already in the car," she said to Kidd.

Alfred nodded and got up immediately. The two boys were soon settled in the back seat of the minivan along with Kidd's sister.

"Seat belts on?" Mom asked.

Kidd helped Alfred put his seat belt strap into the buckle and said, "All systems go."

Kidd's dad started, "Ten, nine, eight..." the others chimed in. By the time they reached three,

Alfred's voice joined the others in the family ritual countdown.

"Blast off!" they all yelled together and the engine was ignited.

On the drive to Playland, Alfred quietly whispered, "Is your mom always so nice?"

"Huh?" Kidd looked at him. "My mom is always this way, why?"

"Dunno, she seems so nice. I thought for sure we were going to get heck for smashing the the robot."

"Naw," Kidd said, "she's used to that. Only when we are having company over, then she wants me to clean up. It's okay, as long as I never leave cars or stuff for her to trip on."

"You're so lucky. My mom is always on my case. I can never leave things out. And if I forget and leave something where she can find it, she throws it in the garbage."

Kidd was shocked. He couldn't imagine his mother doing such a thing.

"She really razzes me to brush my teeth though," Kidd put in quickly, so Alfred wouldn't feel so weird. Alfred nodded in sympathy.

"It must be hard for your mom sometimes," Kidd added. "Hurt people hurt other people. Did you know that?"

"Sure, I knew that," Alfred said with bravado.

"Your mom must be hurting sometimes."

"Huh?" Alfred got quiet for a while, his face reflecting his thoughts. But then he brightened up as he joined in the family fun in the here and now.

At Playland, Alfred was a perfect gentleman. He spent most of his time helping Kidd's little sister play the different games. He was willing to hold her up so she could work the controls and gave her tips on how to score. When they sat down for a rest, he politely volunteered to go with Kidd's dad to get drinks for everyone.

"That Alfred can be quite charming," Kidd's mom said while they were waiting for the refreshments to arrive.

"I like Alfred," Kidd's little sister chimed in. "He's funny."

"He's okay," Kidd agreed.

"I know he gave you lots of trouble earlier this year," Kidd's mom added. "I think you're doing the right thing by befriending him. He seems to be improving. How did you ever come to the idea of making friends with him?"

Kidd thought about telling her about the arrowhead, but he wasn't sure she would understand. He chewed on his bottom lip a moment, then said,

"Maybe it's from learning about history?" He said it like he was guessing, but he knew it was true.

His mother burst out laughing. "You are a funny one." She rubbed the palm of her hand across his cheek. Kidd was afraid she would kiss him, but she just smiled her approval and said, "Here come the drinks."

Why, He Even Gets a Reward from the Teacher

The birthday party was a great success. In the weeks afterward, Alfred and Kidd started to truly become friends. Alfred would often come over to play at Kidd's house and even invited Kidd to his house once in a while. They both agreed after a few visits to Alfred's house that it was easier to play at Kidd's where they didn't have to clean up every time they left the room.

Kidd felt a bit uncomfortable about the way Alfred treated his mother. He was always making faces when she asked him to do something. Alfred would also sneak cookies from the cupboard without permission and then take way too many. It was as if he didn't want to be trusted, or was angry that his mother did not trust him. Kidd wasn't sure which it was, but he didn't like it and felt proud that his own mom always trusted him. She also trusted Alfred the same way, and so Alfred acted differently around her.

In many ways Alfred was changing. But at school Alfred was still bullying some of the smaller kids. Kidd didn't like this and felt uncomfortable when Alfred was mean. One day, not long after talking to the flint about his friend, he decided to do something about it. Alfred was picking on a little girl who had a birthmark, calling her an alien from outer space.

"Alfred," Kidd walked right up to the bigger boy and spoke in a calm, quiet voice. "Can I talk to you for a minute?"

Alfred grinned and said, "Sure." He wagged a finger at the little girl who was nearly in tears and drawled warningly, "I'll...be...back."

Kidd walked all the way across the school playground to the fence where no one else was around. After some humming and hawing for a few minutes, Alfred ordered Kidd to spill the beans and tell him what was on his mind.

"It's when you tease the other kids, the little ones who can't defend themselves," Kidd started. He looked at Alfred, who was listening intently. Encouraged, Kidd went on. "Well, I don't like to be around you when you do that."

Alfred's face started to cloud over with anger. Kidd could see his friend's neck getting redder.

"Hey," Kidd went on. "I still want to be your friend. I still want to play with you but I don't like to be connected with someone who hurts others. Hurt people hurt other people. Did you know that?"

Alfred nodded, "You told me that before."

Kidd nodded, "Yeah, and when you hurt other people, they might go and hurt someone else, and then that person will hurt others, and then…"

"Oh…"

"So when you get into a mood where you bully the other kids, I want you to know that I won't hang around. Okay?"

Alfred's face still looked angry, but also sad. He twitched his nose and sniffed. "Some friend you are," he grumbled, but the bluster of a few minutes ago was gone.

The bell rang and the boys ran hard across the playing field towards the school.

Kidd was afraid that Alfred would start bullying him again, but that didn't happen. Since Alfred wanted to spend time with Kidd, he got to bullying less and less. In fact, he seemed to change in a lot of ways. Some of the other kids started following Kidd's lead and were nicer to Alfred. Even in school, Alfred seemed to make more effort, was quieter in class and paid attention to the teachers.

Why, he even got a reward for being the most improved student in the class! He was so proud of that reward. He took it home to show his mom. Kidd was with him when Alfred burst into the kitchen with the certificate in his hands.

"Look what I got," he yelled out excitedly.

Alfred's mom looked up from where she was busy with some schoolwork of her own. Alfred had told Kidd she was going to night school to improve things.

"Let me see," she said. She looked the certificate over and nodded. Then she looked at her son and scowled. "It's about time you smartened up." She dropped the certificate on the floor and walked out of the room.

Alfred picked up the paper and wiped the dirt from it. He sighed. "Let's go over to your house," he whispered.

The two boys ran over to Kidd's house with the certificate. Alfred burst in the door and flapped the paper in front of Kidd's mother.

"What do you have there, Alfred?" she said. She wiped her hands on her apron because she had been mixing up cookie dough. Kidd's little sister was helping her. Together they looked at the paper that Alfred handed her.

She read the certificate out loud and then said, "Well, that is wonderful. I am so proud of you." She gave Alfred a pat on the shoulder and gave each of the boys a fresh hot cookie from the cooling rack on the counter. "Your mother will be so proud of you," she added.

"Naw," Alfred said with a mouthful of cookie. "She don't care."

"Doesn't care," Kidd's mom corrected automatically.

"Doesn't care," Alfred repeated. "Can I put my reward up on the fridge?" He pointed to the already cluttered refrigerator door.

Kidd's mom moved some of the paintings, shifted the coupons, put the shopping list on the counter and made room for the reward. She and Alfred ceremoniously hung up the certificate with a Smokey the Bear magnet.

"Now I can come over and see it whenever I want," Alfred said.

Kidd's mom laughed. "You are such a funny, dear boy." She rummaged in the fridge for a moment and brought out a container of leftover cake icing. With great pomp she spread icing over another cookie and said, "In honor of his great achievement, I bestow upon Alfred this special cookie."

Everyone laughed and applauded.

Uncle Stan, You Have Been Told!

On Saturday afternoon, Uncle Stan and Aunt Melanie came over. Uncle Stan wanted to borrow a circular saw because they were doing some renovations in their basement. Kidd's dad and Uncle Stan went out to the workshop where the tools were kept. Kidd and his little sister tagged along.

While Dad explained the particulars of the saw to Uncle Stan, Kidd paid close attention so that he would know how to use it when he was old enough. Afterwards, everyone trouped out to a picnic table under the apple tree. The shade of the big old tree was nice. Kidd liked to look at the little apples as they grew. He marveled at how they started out green and hard as nuts but became wonderful, juicy apples in the fall.

As the men were talking, Kidd's mom and her sister brought out glasses and a pitcher of lemonade. Aunt Melanie commented on the wonderful old apple tree.

"You don't see many of them any more," said Uncle Stan. "They are all being replaced by the new dwarf varieties."

"We thought about cutting it down, because it's so much work to keep up, with the pruning and using ladders to pick in the fall," Kidd's dad replied.

"But I wouldn't let him," put in Kidd's mom. "It's a fine old tree and it's sad that most of them are gone now."

"Some of the new apple varieties are very tasty, though, don't you think?" said Aunt Melanie.

"Things change."

"Indeed they do."

Uncle Stan started to tease Kidd's sister. She laughed and teased him back. Then Uncle Stan picked her up and started to twirl her around above his head. Kidd could see that she was hanging on very hard and seemed scared of being dropped. She didn't enjoy it nearly as much as Uncle Stan did. In fact, it seemed that she didn't like it at all.

Kidd looked his uncle right in the eye as the big man paused for breath. He said, "Uncle Stan, sir, I don't think she likes to be twirled around that way. I know that I don't."

Everyone fell silent. A real silence, not just imagined. Kidd thought that he was going to be in trouble for saying what he did. Then Aunt Melanie burst into laughter.

"Well, Stanley," she said boisterously, "you have been told. For years I've been trying to tell him that children don't like to be manhandled that way."

Mom and Dad started to laugh as Aunt Melanie laughed again.

Uncle Stan blushed from the base of his neck to his ears. He put Kidd's sister on the ground and helped her to smooth out her clothes. Sheepishly, he said, "I clean forgot they had feelings. Those little ones are so light and easy to lift. I guess I haven't let go of all of my football tackle mentality. That's what Melanie keeps telling me."

With one eyebrow raised, he looked down the point of his nose at Kidd. He said, "And I remember a time when you paid me back for tackling you." He gave Kidd a playful wink.

Everyone laughed again, even Uncle Stan. Though embarrassed by the old painful memory, Kidd was relieved that he wasn't in trouble, and he felt proud of himself for sticking up for his sister. She stood behind him for the rest of Uncle Stan and Aunt Melanie's visit.

Most of the time Kidd didn't pay much attention to his sister. But after all, she was his sister, and still so little—someone had to stick up for her. Inside himself, he also felt like he had stood up for himself when he was little like her. The awful feelings he'd always had about Uncle Stan were somehow less painful. He felt that he was more in charge of himself—more grown up.

 # One of Those Really Big Gopher Holes

A few days later, Kidd told the arrowhead what he had said to Uncle Stan. Then he added, "And I was really scared for my sister, because I was afraid she might wet herself like I had. I still feel yucky inside about that."

"That is one of those really big gopher holes, isn't it?" the flint asked.

Kidd nodded. "Yes, I felt so bad then, like I was a baby again, and everyone laughed at me."

"And it hurt a lot."

Kidd could feel the sting in his eyes. "It was like Uncle Stan didn't think I was a person. It was as if he didn't know I had feelings. I didn't like that." Kidd thought for a moment. "You said hurt people hurt other people. Do you think Uncle Stan was hurt?"

"Maybe."

"Yeah, maybe when he played football. He was a professional once. Did you know that? A long time ago. Then he got hurt...Oh! So...maybe then?"

"Sometimes the way we live changes the way we act. Then, we forget how to act at other times. Maybe your uncle had people who pushed and whirled him around. Being pushy was part of his job and he thought that was the way he was supposed to treat others."

"Kinda like he learned a pushy wisdom..."

"Yeah, kinda like that. His hurt made him forget about knowing how other people want to be treated."

"Oh...yeah," Kidd said, still not too sure.

That night Kidd had a dream. He dreamed that he was in the field filled with gopher holes. The arrow maker was there and so was Black Raven Alfred. His Uncle Stan was there too, trying to play football but constantly tripping on his gopher holes. The arrow maker went to Uncle Stan and told him to fill in the holes.

"But how can I do that?" Uncle Stan demanded crossly.

The arrow maker told him about beliefs and about that part of him that had been there from the beginning. "First clear the beliefs that get in the way and, as you handle the hurt by filling in those gopher holes, then you will be able to attend to the other beliefs."

"But it's important to have anger and to feel afraid," Uncle Stan said. "That is how I survived playing pro ball."

"And as you fill in the gopher holes and heal the pain and hurt, you will gain the wisdom to know how much to be afraid. You will know the difference between what is possible and what is probable."

Uncle Stan nodded and started filling in gopher holes.

In the dream, Alfred was filling holes too. He was telling his mother about gopher holes, and she was getting less angry with everyone as she learned to fill gopher holes.

The gopher field in Kidd's dream got enormous, as though he could see everywhere and everyone at once. Everyone around him was learning from the others and beginning to fill in holes. Soon all the holes in the field were being filled in. Some of the really big holes were taking more time. Some people were helping others with their bigger hurts, letting them fill in bits at a time, then resting and getting to know each other better. Somehow, newcomers learned to fill in gopher holes in the same mysterious way.

Sure, there were new gopher holes being made. It's not a perfect world. Painful things happen. There was still hurt and pain and fear and anger creating new gopher holes. Some were pretty yucky memories too. But within everyone was a part that was there from the beginning that could fill in gopher holes, turning the painful memories into wisdom. People came to know this wisdom, a wisdom passed down from generation to generation, to each and every person.

Kidd woke up feeling good inside. For a moment, he thought about Alfred and Uncle Stan. He closed his eyes again to look at the dream. The good feeling was still inside him.

"Maybe if I think it, then...maybe it will get to be true," he whispered to himself before falling back to sleep.

Things Change

Over the next while, Kidd came quite a few times to discuss things with the flint. He liked hearing stories of the arrow maker and his people. As time went on, the two spent less time talking about Kidd's life and more about the way things were when the arrow maker was around.

"Things change," the arrowhead said one day. "Things change all the time. Have you noticed how you've changed?"

Kidd crouched down by the tree where the arrowhead lay. The ground around the tree now showed a lot of wear from the scuffing of Kidd's shoes. Kidd plucked a leaf from the nearby bush and fiddled with it as he thought. After a moment he nodded.

"It's about the 'what ifs' that I used to think about," Kidd replied. "I'm starting to figure things out for myself and look at things differently. When a 'what if' comes up, I look at it in the here and now, like you do."

The arrowhead grunted in agreement. "I've noticed you do even more than that."

Kidd thought a moment, and then his face brightened. "I do, too. I try to see the difference between the possibility of what I am afraid of actually happening and the probability." He nodded to himself. "I'm learning to question if it could happen, and then wondering if it ever has happened. Lots of times my 'what ifs' are possible but not probable. They don't actually become real."

"And what good is all that?" the arrowhead asked in his gruff way.

"Well, it means my feelings—you know, feeling scared or angry or even happy—they aren't just feelings that get in the way. I can use them. I'm learning to use my feelings in the here and now to keep myself safe and out of trouble, most of the time."

The arrowhead laughed. "Most of the time. It would be a terrible loss to the world if little boys didn't get into trouble some of the time."

Kidd laughed too, and then shared a story of how he and Alfred were out picking berries in the forest one day and discovered a wasp's nest. They ran very fast and never got stung once. Their fear had made their feet run faster than ever.

"Things change," the arrowhead said again as their laughter died down. "There will come a time when you discover you don't need to come to talk to me any longer."

Kidd started to object.

"No, no—just listen. It is already beginning. You now carry the wisdom within you and there will come a time when it will be your turn to share it with others. This too has begun. You know it to be the truth. And when this comes to pass, you will know that it is well and good."

The arrowhead fell silent in a way that Kidd now recognized. It was time to go and play with the other kids. He knew he could come back any time if he wanted to talk to the arrowhead. He also knew what the arrowhead said was true—things change.

As the summer months passed, Kidd came less and less often to the spot in the forest under the big tree where the piece of flint lay. Eventually he became so busy that he didn't go to see the tiny arrowhead very much at all. Sometimes when he was at the fort, he would look over at the tree under which the arrowhead lay. When he did this, he felt good inside knowing he didn't need to go and talk, and that it was okay not to visit. The arrowhead would understand that he was busy with life the way it was supposed to be, in the here and now. Whenever he saw an actual gopher hole in the area around the play fort, he would imagine filling it in, and he would think of the story of Black Raven. Now he understood how the angry boy had become such a great warrior, because Alfred had become such a great friend.

Alfred could still become angry and mean when someone hurt him, but Kidd never held it against him. He would just stay out of the way and not get involved. Afterwards he would be Alfred's friend, listen to his hurt, and share some of the wisdom of the arrow maker.

Alfred, too, shared wisdom with Kidd. Alfred was very good at knowing when it wasn't safe to be around someone. Alfred would say, "Let's get out of here," and they would go. Many times, he saved Kidd from getting hurt or into trouble. Sometimes when Kidd didn't see the problems coming, Alfred did. There were even times when Alfred didn't have to say much to share his wisdom. They just connected.

The two boys spent a great deal time together. They shared many good memories and Kidd thought they would probably be friends forever. This amazed him, considering how much he hated Alfred in the beginning when he was so often hurt by him. Things change.

The Storm and the Flood

In the history of stone and the history of mountains, change takes place over thousands of years. Time is marked on a much slower scale than it is for the lives of individual people. But when changes do occur to the mountains and the stone, the events can happen with the same sudden speed as they do anywhere.

A giant storm rose out over the ocean hundreds of miles away from the little valley where the huge boulder sat suspended over the children's fort. This storm was unusual, for it grew and grew until it gathered to a very great intensity. The storm was blown by the prevailing winds across the coastal mountains where it dropped a torrent of rain in places where such heavy rains happened all the time and the water ran harmlessly back towards the ocean.

But the strength of this storm was not worn down by the peaks of the coast range, and the moisture-laden clouds moved into the interior towards the high mountain under which the giant boulder sat. Normally, this valley didn't get much rain, but this time it was different. The huge wet storm got snagged on the peaks above the valley where Kidd and Alfred lived. It rained hard for what seemed forever. The boys spent many days indoors looking out the windows and wishing they could go out and play. Puddles grew to a colossal size, but it was too cold to enjoy them. Everyone commented on the unusual weather and the amount of rain.

High up on the mountain the little drops of rain gathered to become puddles too. These puddles overflowed and ran down the sides of the mountain to join with others that became streams of fast flowing, muddy water. But because this was not a normal storm, the water didn't follow the usual watercourses. Instead, the water started to make new routes down the steep sides of the mountain.

As the flow of water gained strength, bits of earth and small rocks were carried with the current. Larger branches and some of the trunks of fallen trees were swept along until they became jammed between the narrow walls of a gully. The gully happened to be directly above the boulder that was balanced over the valley, the very same gully the boulder had bounced down so long ago.

The jammed logs and debris built up until the water became dammed. The water got deeper and deeper in the gully. The branches and old logs could barely hold back the growing weight of the water rushing down from above. Suddenly the dam broke and a wall of mud crashed through the dam to plunge down the gully, gathering more debris as it went.

This flood struck the boulder and split to flow on either side of the huge rock. Bit by bit, the water washed away the earth and pebbles around the base. Larger stones began to give way, and the balance of the massive rock started to shift. It was almost imperceptible at first, but slowly, pulled by the forces of gravity, the momentum of the great stone grew to where it began to roll. Smaller boulders joined in a crashing tumble down the slope.

The huge rock bounced down, smacking from one tree to the next. Tree trunks shattered from the force and caused the rock to change directions this way and that, so no one could have predicted its path. Its momentum was very great. When it reached the flat where the child's fort lay, it struck one corner of the log structure but didn't stop, only changing direction to roll down the trail upon which Kidd and his friends walked nearly every day.

The huge rock channeled for a short distance on the trail, like a marble on a marble run, and then with a loud shuddering crash, it hit the edge of a tree trunk and was dumped off the beaten path. It struck one last tree before coming to rest. All was

silent again in the forest except for the echo of the
flooding waters in the creek.

 # Never Would Kidd Have Thought of That!

After the rains stopped, the children all came out to play in the puddles. The little children liked running in and out of the wet in the rubber boots that they usually wore in winter. The bigger kids were busy trying to make boats and rafts to float stuff in the middle of the "lakes." More than one fashion doll and miniature truck were lost to the depths of the puddles. They wouldn't be found until the rainwater dried up later in the week.

Kidd decided to hike up to the fort to see what was happening. He was a bit worried that the rains from the storm might have washed away the leaves covering the arrowhead. If that happened, the arrowhead would no longer be safely hidden. On the way to the fort he was amazed at the damage the rainwater had created. Trees had fallen down, some across the path so that he had to scramble over them. Great ruts carved by flowing water, now nearly dried up, cut through a steep section of the trail. Bare rocks and tree roots were exposed, making it hard to walk. He had to pay attention so he wouldn't slip and fall.

Kidd noticed the smashed edge of the fort first.

"Oh no!" he cried out. "We worked so hard to get those logs into place!" Now they were smashed and pushed aside like giant pick-up sticks.

He started to run towards the fort but then he looked up and saw the giant boulder was gone, no where to be seen. Stopped in his tracks, he scanned the slope above the fort, letting his gaze follow the path of the boulder. He could tell where it had traveled by the destruction left behind. Big trees were broken off, the trunks shattered into long strands of wood, and the rock had gouged out holes in the turf of the flat land as it continued on its route. It had rolled down the trail past where he was standing. Turning, he looked back the way he had come.

Everything had changed so much that he didn't realize that he'd walked past the tree where the piece of flint lay. A huge breath was expelled from his body as he saw where the boulder lay, off to the side of the trail. The uppermost branches of a very familiar bush were sticking out from under the crushing force of the big rock.

"No!" Kidd gasped.

What if that boulder came down and landed on the arrowhead?

Not in a million years would Kidd have believed that! The tree seemed so far away from where the boulder had originally sat above the fort. But that was precisely what happened.

The shock was beginning to settle in as Kidd examined the tree that had grown above the flint. He looked at how the bark and some of the wood had been torn away by the rock. Underneath the gigantic silent stone, somewhere, lay a dead dried-up worm, some leaves and a small hut of branches. Under that was the arrowhead.

Kidd remembered how the arrow maker had breathed the wisdom into the arrowhead, how he had breathed from the four directions. He leaned against the edge of the big rock and shut his eyes. He could see the arrow maker in his mind and beyond him the eldest of the elders nodding in understanding and wisdom. The arrowhead was now protected by this massive stone; a stone that had come from the same rock wall high up on the mountain peak.

"Hey, are you there?" Kidd called out, halfheartedly tapping on the damaged trunk of the tree. Hope wavered momentarily, but he knew he wouldn't hear that gruff voice answer.

In the certainty of that silence, sadness settled over him. He felt a loss, and he was confused, but he also had a sense that things were the way they should be. He knew that he would never be able to talk to the arrowhead again. He wiped away a single tear that slipped down his face. It had come full circle. Like the arrowhead said, things change.

"And when this comes to pass, know that it is well and good," the voice of the arrowhead almost seemed to echo through the forest. Kidd only heard the silence, but the words were in his heart.

As Kidd looked up at the enormous rock, he marveled at how truly large it was now that it was close. He noticed that the rough edges would allow him to climb up. Scrambling to the crest, he surveyed the trail and the fort. In the distance, he could even glimpse the rooftops of the houses in the town where he grew up. It was the same town in which his grandfather had grown up; the town his great, great, great grandfather had helped to create as a pioneer.

Kidd thought about growing up. Someday he would have kids and then one day, he too would be a grandfather. In his mind he could see himself coming up here with his grandchildren. He would tell them the story of the arrowhead under the huge rock. He smiled. They might not believe him at first, but then again they might. Children often have a type of wisdom that is lost in adulthood.

Kidd closed his eyes and remembered those first moments with the flint. He could almost hear the story again. That guiding voice, which had become so familiar, now seemed to come from within. He knew that the wisdom he had learned would be with him forever. He mustered a smile. He could teach that knowledge to his children and his grandchildren—the same way his grandfather had taught him of horse manure and the growing of roses.

It was wisdom that had been passed on from generation to generation, from the very beginning of all knowledge. It was wisdom from the four directions of anywhere on earth.

Further Reading

Callahan, R. (2006). Books, CDs, and materials available from http://www.tftrx.com

Craig, G. (2006). Books, CDs, and materials available from http://www.emofree.com

Flint, G. A. (2001). *Emotional Freedom: Techniques for dealing with emotional and physical distress.* NeoSolTerric Enterprises: Vernon, British Columbia.

Flint, G. A. (2006). *A Theory and Treatment of Your Personality: a manual for change.* NeoSolTerric Enterprises: Vernon, British Columbia.

About the Authors

Garry A. Flint, a practicing clinical psychologist, and Jo C. Willems, an artist and writer, share a deep compassion and drive to understand the human condition. Their diverse  gifts create a blend of inspiration and creativity that has led to a productive collaboration. Educated at Indiana University (1968), Dr. Flint has a unique understanding of how the human personality works. His clinical practice and his many publications reflect this understanding. Dual degrees in Microbiology and Fine Art amplify the artistic imagination of Jo C. Willems (B.Sc., UBC, 1975; MFA, UC, Irvine, 1978). Lively discussions on memory theory, art perception, and even grammar have been a part of Garry and Jo's regular lunchtime meetings for more than a decade. Both authors have committed themselves to finding effective ways to help people change and grow.

To Purchase

A Healing Legend:
Wisdom from the Four Directions
Purchase from:
- Barnes & Noble
- Bookstores through Ingram or Baker & Taylor
- Amazon.com

Emotional Freedom: Techniques for dealing with emotional and physical distress
Purchase from:
- Book Clearing House:
  Telephone: 1 800 431-1579 (24 hours)
- Bookstores through Ingram or Baker & Taylor
- Amazon.com

A Theory and Treatment of Your Personality: a manual for change
Purchase from:
- Barnes & Noble
- Bookstores through Ingram or Baker & Taylor
- Amazon.com

Printed in the United States
88287LV00001B/112/A